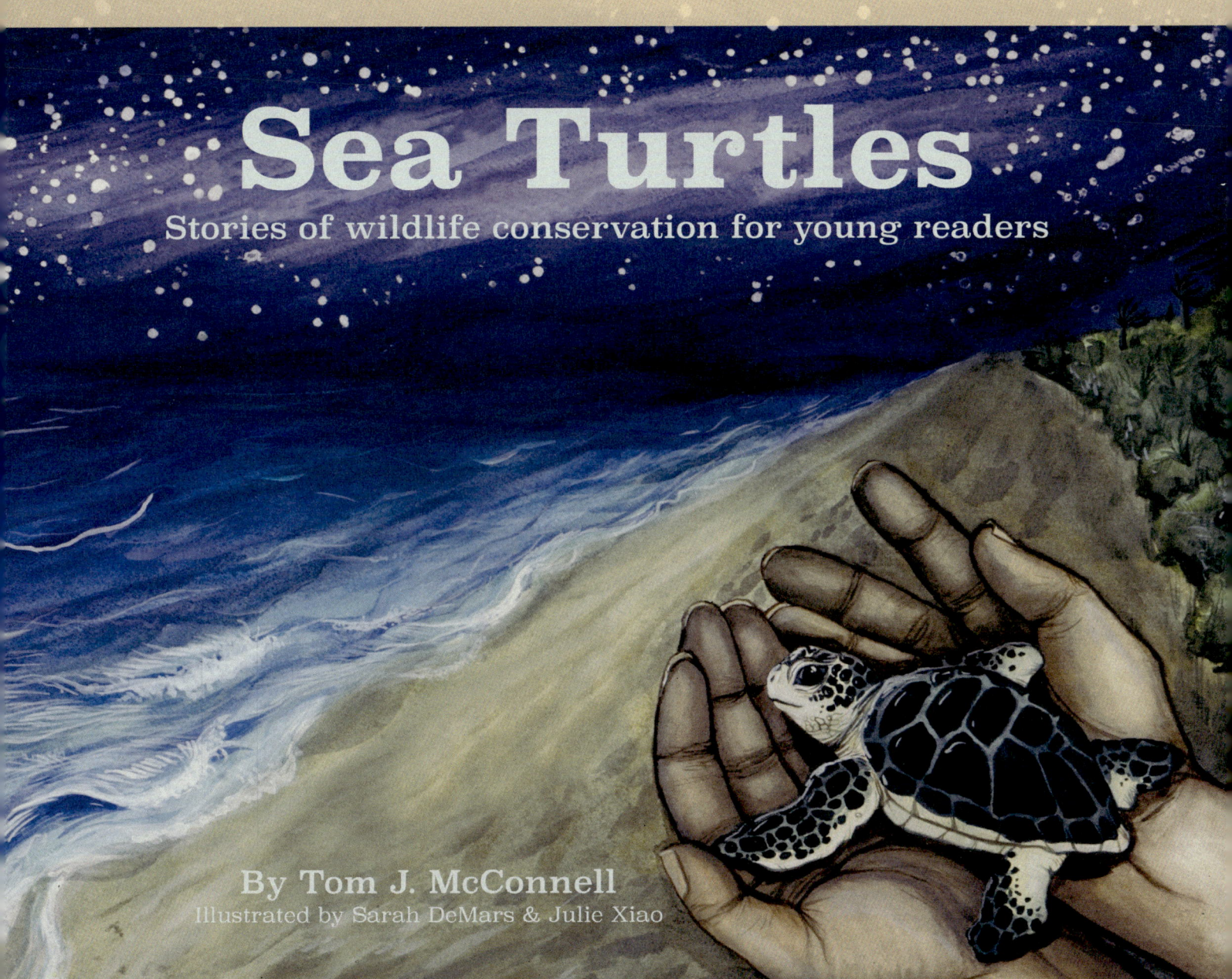

CONSERVATION TALES

Sea Turtles

Stories of wildlife conservation for young readers

By Tom J. McConnell
Illustrated by Sarah DeMars & Julie Xiao

Airway Publishing

Conservation Tales: Sea Turtles

Copyright © 2018 Ball State University.
All rights reserved.

Author: Tom J. McConnell
Educational Activity Writer: Rebecca Tripp
Publisher: Airway Publishing, Muncie, Indiana, USA
Illustrations: Sarah DeMars & Julie Xiao
Graphic Design: Kendra Schemmel
Printed by CreateSpace

46 p

No part of this publication may be reproduced or distributed in any form or by any means, or stored in a database or retrieval system, without the prior written consent of the author, including, but not limited to, networked or other electronic storage or transmission, or broadcast for distance learning.

ISBN-13 # 978-0-9863369-9-7

For the many teachers who helped instill in me a love of nature, a desire to learn, and the drive to aim high and persist. Special thanks to Bill Brenneman, Bob Turner, and Carl Weaver.

Tom McConnell

To my mom and dad, who have lovingly supported me throughout the beginning of my artistic career. I love you. And to Tom, who introduced me to children's book illustration. Your fascination with biology and conservation is contagious and inspiring!

Sarah DeMars

To my family, friends and teachers who are always pushing me past my comfort zone and to stay ambitious. To God for leading me to Barb and Tom, who allowed me to connect my love for nature and design to educate and initiate change in the world. Special thanks to my godmother, Patricia Selhorst, who has been guiding me through spirit my entire life, I couldn't do it without you!

Kendra Schemmel

Hannah and her family were walking along the sandy beach. She and her brother, Ezekiel, really liked looking for sea shells at the water's edge.

As they explored, Hannah noticed an area in the sand marked off with wooden posts and yellow tape. There was a woman wearing a Mote Marine Laboratory and Aquarium shirt, with caution tape in her hand, standing near the nest.

Hannah ran toward the posts. "I want to see what this is!"

"Yeah, me too!" Ezekiel raced after her.

"Don't touch when you get there," their mom said. "We're coming too."

Hannah ran up close to the sign. It had two pictures of a sea turtle and said "Do Not Disturb - Sea Turtle Nest."

As they looked at the sign, the woman with the bucket said, "You can look, but please do not cross the yellow tape. We do not want anyone to disturb the turtle eggs."

"Turtle eggs?" Ezekiel cried. "That's so cool! What kind of turtles?"

"This nest was made by a loggerhead turtle," the woman told him. "The eggs were laid about sixty days ago, and they could hatch any day now."

"Is that why you are here?" Hannah asked. By this time their parents had caught up with them and were listening, too.

"Yes, it is! My name is Melissa and I am a scientist who studies sea turtles. We check the nests each day to make sure they are not disturbed. We have a group of volunteers who live near here that help watch and protect the nests, too."

Hannah asked, "Protect them? From what?"

"Well, there are a lot of things. Sometimes people drive equipment on the sand or dig to see the eggs, and that can harm them. There are also animals like raccoons, armadillos and coyotes that will try to eat the eggs, and we want to prevent that." Melissa replied.

"Wow! So do you stay here all day and night?" asked Hannah.

Melissa laughed. "Well, no. But this neighborhood has a lot of volunteers who take turns here. They check the nests each day."

Ezekiel perked up, "I think sea turtles are really neat, but I have never seen a sea turtle nest before. How many eggs do they have?"

"And how do their babies get out of the nest? I heard they have to crawl all the way back to the water." Hannah squeezed past her brother to get Melissa's attention.

Melissa smiled. "I am glad you are both interested in sea turtles. The baby turtles have to dig their way to the surface. If you come back in about three days, you can watch as we open one of the nests that hatched today to see what is left after the turtles hatch."

Hannah jumped up and down. "Mom, can we come back? I would really like to see that!"

Hannah's mom, Kathy, looked down at her daughter.
"Sure! I would like to see it too! We can plan to be here."

Kemp's ridley turtle

Loggerhead turtle

When they got home. Hannah and Ezekiel ran inside to find some books about sea turtles. They looked for the kinds of turtles that nest where they live.

In the books, they saw pictures of loggerhead turtles, green turtles, hawksbill turtles, and Kemp's ridley turtles. The pictures were interesting. Hannah had a hard time figuring out how to tell the sea turtles apart. The book said some of the turtles are endangered, and that others are threatened. Endangered means they could go extinct if we don't help them. Threatened means they are rare enough that they need protection.

"Mom, which turtles are threatened or endangered?" Ezekiel looked up from the book he was flipping through.

Hannah chimed in, "Do all the turtles come here at the same time? And why are they endangered?"

"I am not sure, kids" her mom said. "Why don't you look it up online? Or we can ask Melissa when we see her in a few days."

Green turtle

Hawksbill turtle

Three days later, Hannah and her family drove back to the beach. The sun was just rising over the ocean when they saw a couple of volunteers standing near the nesting site.

As soon as they saw Melissa, Hannah and Ezekiel ran over to her.

"Welcome back!" Melissa said. "I am glad that you decided to come watch. Just make sure you stand back."

Hannah's mom spread some beach towels on the sand and they sat to watch. They noticed that Melissa and her friend were both wearing shirts that said Mote on the back.

"I wonder how the aquarium is going to help with the baby turtles." Hannah thought to herself.

After about 20 minutes, the team had finished digging up the nest. They found lots of hatched turtle egg shells, and even a few rotten eggs. Hannah was most excited when they found a few baby turtles that were still alive! The team from Mote put the little turtles in a red bucket.

"Where are you taking the turtles?" Ezekiel asked.

"These little guys were too weak to make it out of their nest," Melissa explained. "We let most of them go back to the wild right away. We take the ones that need some care back to Mote to help them get stronger. Then we release them back into the wild, too."

Scientists and volunteer excavate nests after the eggs hatch. (Mote Marine Laboratory, 2015)

The other woman from the aquarium was writing on a clipboard. Hannah was standing on her tiptoes trying to see what it said.

The woman saw her looking and bent down to show her. "Hi! I'm Kristen. We are counting the eggs that hatched from the nest. We try to do this with all of the nests in the area. We use the numbers each year to find out how many hatchlings came from each beach."

"So you are studying the sea turtles? That is awesome!" Hannah said. "I want to be a scientist who studies sea turtles!"

The children had been to Mote before, but they had never met a turtle researcher until now. They did not know that the scientists at the aquarium come to the beach to study turtle nests.

"That is awesome!" said Ezekiel. "I want to know why the turtles are endangered."

Researchers count number of hatched and unhatched eggs in each nest. (Mote Marine Laboratory, 2015)

Volunteers mark a new nest site. (Florida FWC, 2010)

"You see," said Kristen, "turtles are endangered or threatened because we have disturbed their nesting areas. All these buildings and the lights can make it hard for turtles to find a safe place to lay eggs. Sometimes the baby turtles can't get back to the water because of stuff we leave on the beach, too."

"Oh! And that is why these signs are here, right?" Eekiel asked.

"Yes, it is. We try to protect as many nests as we can," Kristen answered.

Melissa added, "There are other problems, too. Mote rescues a lot of turtles that have been injured. Sometimes turtles get hit by boats or tangled up in fishing gear. We also find turtles that have tumors from a virus. When we find turtles that are sick or injured, we try to help them. Some of them have to come back to our hospital."

Hannah was amazed, "A hospital for sea turtles? I would like to see that!"

"That is where we are taking these baby turtles," Kristen told Hannah. "They need some help to build up their strength. Then we can release them back to the ocean."

Green turtle entangled in fishing net. (NOAA PIFSC 2012)

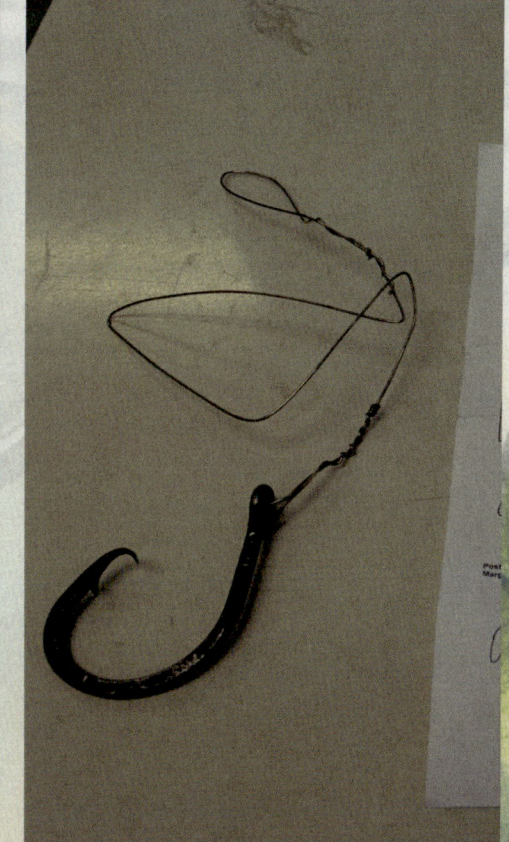

Hook removed from injured turtle. (K. Johnson, 2018)

"So, do you think you would like to come to Mote to see how we take care of the baby turtles that need some help?" Melissa asked.

"Mom, can we go, please!?" Hannah begged.

Hannah's mom shrugged her shoulders, "Sounds interesting. We can check it out."

The next day, Hannah's family loaded up their van and headed over to Mote.

Squirt, a Kemp's ridley turtle (R. Tripp, 2018)

Harry, a green turtle at Mote. (K. Johnson, 2018)

Shelley, a loggerhead turtle at Mote. (McConnell 2018)

When they arrived at Mote, Hannah and Ezekiel wanted to see the sea turtles. On their way into the sea turtle hatchling hospital, they saw Hang Tough, a blind green turtle.

Ezekiel's favorite turtle was a Kemp's ridley turtle named Squirt. Squirt had been hurt by a boat and could no longer live in the wild. A green turtle named Harry swam in a tank with two manatees.

Hannah loved Shelley and Montego, the pair of loggerhead turtles that were raised by humans. Hannah found out that a school in the area had held an essay contest where the winner picked out the turtles' names.

Hatchling hospital at Mote. (K. Johnson, 2018)

While they were looking at the turtles, Melissa came by. Hannah was excited to see her again. "Hey, Melissa! We saw you on the beach! We came to find out more about the baby sea turtles you brought here."

"Hi! I remember you!" Melissa said, "Come over here and you can see the sea turtle hatchling hospital."

Melissa led the children to a window where they could look into the lab. There were small pools with baby sea turtles in them. Through the window, the kids saw a woman feeding some of the turtles. "That's Amber," Melissa said. "She is one of the people who takes care of the turtles."

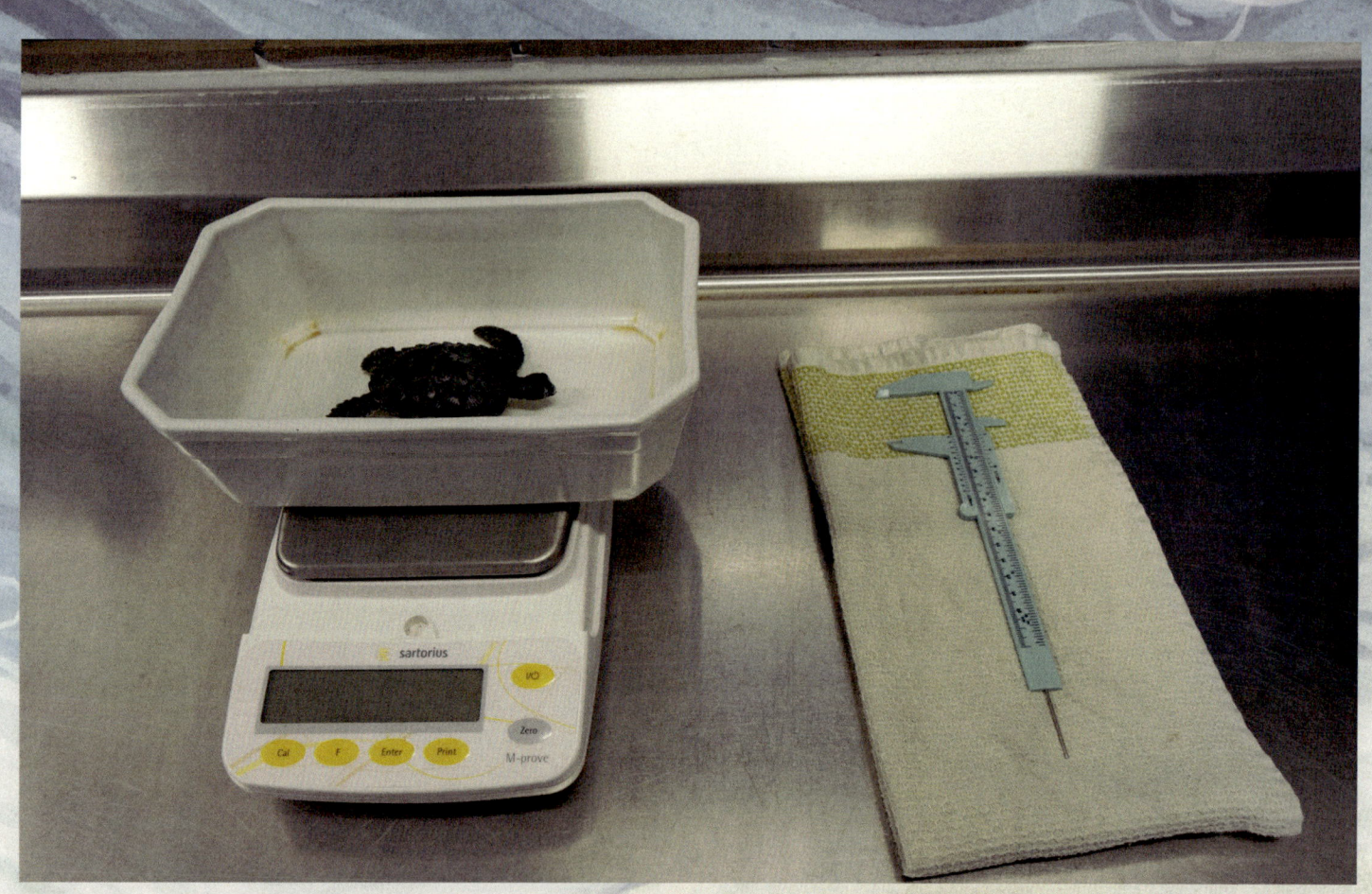

Hatchlings in need of medical care are brought to Mote. (K. Johnson, 2018)

Amber saw the children and came out to meet them. She explained that some baby sea turtles need food to build up enough strength to go back to the ocean. Others were injured and need some medical care.

"How long will they stay here?" Ezekiel asked.

"Most will stay here a few days," Amber explained. "Others need more time to recover. We hope to release all of them as soon as possible. If they are injured too badly to be released, they may end up in aquariums like Hang Tough and Squirt."

Hannah was busy watching the turtles. "You have a lot of baby turtles here! How many babies does each turtle have?"

Amber told her that loggerhead turtles lay about 100 eggs in each nest. "Most females will dig 4 to 7 nests when they breed. The eggs take about two months to hatch. Most of the babies do not survive to be adults. Every baby we can rescue gets a second chance."

Hatchlings emerging from nest.
(AL Bureau of Land Management, 2015)

Sea turtle eggs are the size and shape of ping pong balls. (Deepwater Horizon Response, 2009)

"You have different kinds of turtles here," Hannah asked, "How do you tell what kind they are?"

Amber explained, "Each species of turtle has its own pattern of scales called 'scutes' on their heads and their shells" She pointed to Montego. "See how he has one big scute on the middle of his head? That means he is a loggerhead. Green turtles have two narrow scutes right between their eyes."

She led them to Squirt's tank and pointed, "You can tell by the shape of the shell too. Kemp's ridley turtles like Squirt are very round. But Montego is shaped like an almond."

Ezekiel said, "Yeah! I can see the difference!" He went to see Harry, the green turtle with the manatees, to see about the scutes on his head.

Amber and another trainer working with Squirt, a Kemp's ridley turtle. (K. Johnson, 2018)

Amber looked at her watch. "I'd like to tell you more, but it is time for the turtles to do their training. I have to get ready for that. You are welcome to stay and watch though."

Hannah was excited to see them train the turtles. She was starting to think she might want to be a scientist to help study turtles. She wondered what kind of training they do and wanted to know more about it. "Can we stay and watch them train the turtles, Mom?" she asked.

"Certainly! I want to watch, too," her mom said.

Amber and another woman brought out some containers and something that looked like a plastic table. They came to Squirt's tank. They put the table in the water and held a round sign with a colored spot on it in the water. Lots of people had come to watch, so Hannah and Ezekiel found a place to stand close to the trainers.

Soon, Squirt swam onto the table next to the trainers. They gave the turtle some pieces of squid and fish. They explained to the people watching that they train the turtle to swim onto the shelf so they can do medical exams while the turtle is still in the water. They check the turtle's skin and shell, and sometimes take blood samples.

The trainers also worked with Shelley and Montego, the turtles in the other tank. They explained about their experiments to find out how well sea turtles can hear. They played different kinds of sounds underwater, and they want the turtles to touch colored markers called targets to show they heard the sound.

When the training was done, Hannah had more questions. "You said Squirt lives here because he had an injury from a boat strike. What happens to other turtles that get hurt?" she asked Amber.

Turtles like Shelley are trained to swim to a "target." (K. Johnson, 2018)

"That's a great question, Hannah," Amber said. "Sometimes people call us to report an injured turtle. When that happens, we send a team to rescue the turtle. If we can help the turtle, we bring it back to our hospital. We have several turtles here now recovering from injuries."

Ezekiel asked. "We saw the hatchling hospital. Are the injured turtles here? I didn't see another hospital."

Amber laughed. "Actually, you walked past the hospital as you came into this building. I can show you where it is, but we do not take our visitors there. The turtles need quiet time to help them heal.

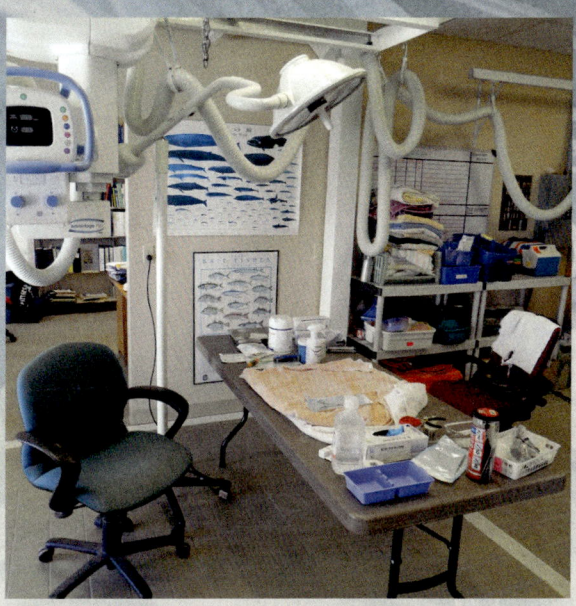

Operating room in Mote's animal hospital.

Recovery tanks in Mote's sea turtle hospital (K. Schemmel, 2018)

Near the entrance to the building, Amber showed them a fenced-in area with big green tanks. "This is our turtle hospital. We have an operating room upstairs, too. When injured turtles are recovering we keep them here until they are well. Then, if possible, we release them again."

Ezekiel asked, "Are all the turtles injured by boats?"

"No, not all of them," Amber said. "We see a lot of turtles who are injured when they get tangled in fishing gear like fishing line and crab traps. Others have swallowed fishing hooks, plastic bags, or other trash. Sometimes we have to do surgery to remove those things."

Mote's rescue and animal care staff help a loggerhead turtle. (C. Goulding/Mote Marine Laboratory, 2018)

Green sea turtle with FPV tumors. (P. Bennet & U. Keuper-Bennet 1992)

Hannah said, "Oh, no! Boats, hooks, trash, fishing line . . . I didn't know we did so much harm to turtles."

Amber told them that not all the turtles in the hospital were hurt by humans. "We also get turtles that have tumors caused by a virus. Most of the time we can remove the tumor, and the turtles will be ok." She showed the kids a poster about the sea turtle virus in the hallway.

Amber pointed to one of the hospital tanks. "That tank has a green turtle that we will release at the beach tomorrow. A scientist will put a radio transmitter on its shell, and it will help us get more data about where turtles go when they are not nesting."

"A radio transmitter? What is that?" Ezekiel asked.

"It is a device like a beeper," Amber told them. "It sends a signal to a satellite to tell us where the turtle is. It lasts about a year, then it falls off. We get the data from the satellite, and share it with other scientists."

Olive ridley sea turtle with a GPS transmitter. (Joanna Gilkeson/USFWS 2017)

As they talked, Hannah and Ezekiel were thinking about what they had learned.

Ezekiel said, "Wow, I did not know how hard it is to be a sea turtle. They have a lot of problems."

"Yeah, they do!" Hannah said. "I'd like to find a way to help sea turtles. Is there anything we can do?"

"Sure! There are a lot of things," Amber told them. "One of the easiest things is to make sure you pick up ALL of your trash if you go to the beach or the park. It is surprising how many people leave their garbage on the sand."

"I saw that Mote quit using plastic straws in their diner to help reduce plastic trash," Hannah's mom mentioned.

"Yes, and we do not have plastic bags or single-use water bottles for the same reason," Amber said. "But there are other things, too. We try to teach fishermen to pick up all their used fishing line and other gear. That is something just about anyone can do to help."

Mote staff released Spock, a loggerhead turtle, after he recovered. (Conor Goulding/Mote Marine Laboratory, 2018)

Volunteer cleaning up the beach. (Leah Oviedo, 2007)

USFWS/Becky Skiba, 2012

Sea turtles sometimes eat plastic bags and straws thinking they are food.

Amber told them about other ways people are helping sea turtles. "In the neighborhoods by the beaches, some people volunteer to help protect nests to keep people and animals from disturbing the eggs."

She continued, "And people in some of those neighborhoods also use red or shielded outdoor lights for their homes. Bright lights can confuse baby sea turtles when they hatch."

"I am glad people that live by the beach are doing things to help turtles," Kathy said.

"Mom, we should do some of this stuff at home," Hannah said. "And I want to learn more about sea turtles! I'd like to be a scientist and help turtles someday."

Ezekiel added, "Yeah! I am going to stop using straws. Maybe we can pick up trash at the beach too!"

Kathy said, "I think that is a great idea. I know we can change how we do some things."

Amber smiled, "That would be great! And I know you would make a great scientist. We have programs at the aquarium for kids who want to learn more or volunteer to help."

38

The next week Hannah and her family went for another walk along the beach. But after learning about sea turtles, they did some things differently. They brought a bucket and picked up litter as they walked. They also brought water in reusable bottles.

"Hey, I see a lot of the things Amber told us about, like the trash people leave on the beach," Hannah said.

"Me, too," said Ezekiel. "I am glad we learned how we can make a difference."

Action Plans

Amber gave Hannah and Ezekiel some brochures with information about sea turtle conservation. Here is a list of things you can do at home, too.

- **Reduce the amount of plastic you use and throw away.** Buy products in biodegradable packaging and recycle any plastics you can. Use refillable water bottles, and a fabric tote bag at the grocery store. Ask restaurants to use paper straws and bags.

- **Take any trash and fishing gear with you when you leave the beach or the park.** When you go fishing, don't leave hooks and used line in or around the water. Wildlife can get entangled or eat it. When you go to the beach bring a bucket or reusable bag to pick up trash so it doesn't get washed into the water.

- **Help protect beaches and wild areas from erosion** from storms and boat wakes. Check with your local parks for volunteer projects to plant native beach grasses and shrubs that help prevent erosion.

- **Reduce your carbon footprint.** Burning coal, oil and gas, or using electricity made from these fuels, contributes to climate change and the acidification of the oceans. Rising oceans erode beachs, and acids damage coral reefs where sea turtles live.

Author's Notes

Dear Reader,

If you're like me you have probably seen sea turtles at a zoo or an aquarium. My first memory of a sea turtle was at an aquarium in Chicago. It was not until 2013 that I saw a sea turtle nest for the first time. That was in Puerto Rico, and it was marked by signs and tape, just like the nest you read about in this story.

It was not until then that I began learning that I could do things to help sea turtles, even though I live far away from an ocean. I have always been interested in helping to protect wildlife and our environment, even when I was very young. Because I care about wildlife, I try to make choices that can help.

The process of writing this book gave me a much closer look at sea turtles. The staff at Mote taught me about the life history of sea turtles, some things about their health and biology, and even how to tell what species of turtle I see. Meeting Shelley, Montego, Squirt and Hang Tough was very special. Even more special was meeting the turtles in the hospital and the people who take care of them. Sea turtles are a lot like many animals – they have an incredible power to recover from injuries. But it is still important to protect the animals and their habitats.

I know that the team that helped to create this book have learned a lot, too. All of us have made changes to some of our daily choices and habits. Many of those ideas are listed in the Conservation Actions. We hope you will think about making similar changes, too. Little things that we can do every day can make a huge difference.

And you can make a difference, too.

Tom J. McConnell, Ph.D.
conservationtales.com

Inquiry Activities

The following activities let you practice some of the skills as sea turtle researchers. To download handouts, view web sites, and more, visit the Learning Links on the Conservation Tales website:
conservationtales.com/sea-turtles

Featured Activity - Sea Turtle Trackers.
Use the link to conserveturtles.org to see real tracking data about sea turtle movements. Download the activity for an inquiry lesson comparing the movement of different turtles.

Other activities

- **Plastic Patrol** – Activity to examine how much plastic you use, and what happens to that plastic.
- **Sea Turtle Energy Pyramid** – Find out how much food a sea turtle needs to understand the importance of protecting their habitats.
- **Turtle Detectives** – Learn to identify sea turtles and the tracks they leave in the sand. Then test your skill at sea turtle identification.

Sea turtle sculpture made of plastic trash. (B. Giorgio-Booher, 2018)

Conservation Tales on the Web

Find out about other books in this series, links to learning resources, and other "extras" at
conservationtales.com

Connections to Standards

Teachers and Homeschoolers -

The table below shows the alignment of concepts and activities in this book with the Next Generation Science Standards (NGSS Lead States, 2013). Each Performance Expectation is a learning objective that reflects a Science and Engineering Practice in the context of a specific Disciplinary Core Idea that falls within a broad Crosscutting Concept. Connections to the Common Core State Standards and the Nature of Science are also listed in the yellow sections of the table.

Performance Expectations	Disciplinary Core Ideas	Science & Engineering Practices	Crosscutting Concepts
3-LS4-2: Use evidence to construct an explanation for how the variations in characteristics among individuals of the same species may provide advantages in surviving, finding mates, and reproducing. **3-LS4-3:** Construct an argument with evidence that in a particular habitat some organisms can survive well, some survive less well, and some cannot survive at all. **3-5-ETS1-1:** Define a simple design problem reflecting a need or a want that includes specified criteria for success and constraints on materials, time, or cost. **3-5-LS4-4:** Make a claim about the merit of a solution to a problem caused when the environment changes and the types of plants and animals that live there change. **5-LS2-1:** Develop a model to describe the movement of matter among plants, animals, decomposers, and the environment.	**LS2.A:** Interdependent Relationships in Ecosystems **LS2B:** Cycles of Matter and Energy Transfer in Ecosystems **LS2C:** Ecosystem Dynamics, Functioning and Resilience **LS4.B:** Natural Selection **LS4.C:** Adaptation **LS4.D:** Biodiversity and Humans	Asking Questions and Defining Problems Planning and Carrying Out Investigations Analyzing and Interpreting Data Constructing Explanations and Designing Solutions	Patterns Cause and Effect System and System Models Stability and Change
		Common Core State Standards Connections	**Connections to the Nature of Science**
		ELA/Literacy - RI.3.1; RI.3.2; RI.3.3; W.3.1; W.3.2; SL.3.8; SL.3.4 *Mathematics –* MP.2; MP.4; MP.5; 3.MD.B.3; 3.MD.8.4	Science Models, Laws, Mechanisms, and Theories Explain Natural Phenomena Scientific Knowledge Assumes an Order and Consistency in Natural Systems

NGSS Lead States. 2013. *Next Generation Science Standards: For states, by states*. Washington, DC: National Academies Press. www.nextgenscience.org

Meet Our Team

Tom J. McConnell, Ph.D., is an associate professor of Science Education in the Department of Biology, Ball State University. Dr. McConnell's teaching and research interests focus on inquiry science teaching.

Rebecca Tripp is an Elementary Education student with a Reading concentration. In addition to helping develop the story, she assists in creating learning activities and outreach materials.

Illustrator
Sarah DeMars studies animation and illustration at Ball State. She also illustrated the *Salamanders* book, and has experience with both digital and traditional media.

Illustrator
Julie Xiao joined the team in Spring 2018 as a illustrator. She is an animation major at Ball State University, and works as an freelance artist on some independent projects.

Graphic Designer
Kendra Schemmel is a graphic designer at Ball State. She also contributes to the development of promotional and educational materials for the Conservation Tales.

Photographer
Kyra Johnson is a photography student at Ball State University. She is excited to use her love of nature and photography to help contribute to the books.

Published by Airway Publishing.
Printed by CreateSpace.

Photo Credits

Photos provided by the author and content consultants except for images from Creative Commons sources. The following lists credits from the owners of the additional images.

Page	Source	License
13	Mote Marine Laboratory	By permission
15	Mote Marine Laboratory	By permission
16	Florida FWC	CC 20
17	NOA PIFSC	CC 2.0
23	Deepwater Horizon Response	CC 2.0
23	AL Bureau of Land Management	CC 2.0
30	Conor Goulding/Mote Marine Laboratory	By permission
31	Peter Bennet & Ursula Keuper-Bennet	CC 3.0
33	Joanna Gilkeson/USFWS	Public Domain
35	Leah Oviedo	CC 2.0
35	USFWS/Becky Skiba	CC 2.0
35	Conor Goulding/Mote Marine Laboratory	By permission

CC 2.0 - Creative Commons license v. 2.0. See https://creativecommons.org/licenses/by/2.0/

For complete listing of licenses and URLs, view author contact info at **conservationtales.com**

Art Director Barbara Giorgio-Booher and Author Tom J. McConnell

Acknowledgments

Content Consultants
Mote Marine Laboratory & Aquarium - Amber Shaw, Melissa Bernhard, Kristen Mazzarella, Lynn Byrd

Art Direction
Barbara Giorgio-Booher, MFA

Illustrations
Sarah DeMars
Julie Xiao

Graphic Design
Kendra Schemmel

Photography
Kyra Johnson, Rebecca Tripp, Kendra Schemmel

Educational Consultants
Cera Foote, Ball State Univ.
Caitlin Zonder, Avon, IN

Additional Photography
Mote Marine Laboratory & Aquarium

Special Thanks to Pamela Siderski, Community Relations Director at Mote Marine Laboratory, and all the staff and volunteers at Mote.

Support for the publication of this book provided by the College of Sciences and Humanities, the School of Art, the Office of Immersive Learning, and the Create Program, Ball State University.

Made in the USA
Middletown, DE
03 July 2018